NATURE EXPLORER

by Paul Sterry

RUNNING PRESS
KIDS
PHILADELPHIA·LONDON

Paul Sterry earned his Ph.D. degree in zoology. Director of a natural history photographic agency, he has written several books for children and adults.

QUARTO CHILDREN'S BOOKS

This book was designed and produced by
Quarto Children's Books Ltd

First published in the United States in 1995 by Running Press Book Publishers. This edition published in 2005 in the United States by Running Press Kids, an imprint of Running Press Book Publishers
125 South Twenty-second Street
Philadelphia, Pennsylvania 19103-4399

Manufactured and printed in China

10 9 8 7 6 5 4 3 2 1
Digit on the right indicates the number of this printing.

Library of Congress Control Number:
2003111203

ISBN   0-7624-1846-X

Colors or contents may vary from those illustrated.

This book may be ordered by mail from the publisher.
Please include $2.50 for postage and handling.
But try your bookstore first!

Visit us on the web!
www.runningpress.com

PICTURE ACKNOWLEDGMENTS:
Key: r = right, l = left, c = center, t = top, b = bottom. Where several pictures are grouped they are numbered in Roman numerals, left to right, then top to bottom. Named pictures appear in the animal identifiers.
Quarto Publishing would like to thank Nature Photographers Ltd for the supply of all photographs. All by Paul Sterry except: S. C. Bisserot: 13 briii, 21 bl; I. Bowen: Bettle Larva; N. Brown: 13 bri, 13 briv, 16 brii, Mayfly Nymph, Springtail; R. Brush: 9 tl; N. A. Callow: 8 bi, 8 biii, 29 cl, Harvestman, Mite; C. Carver: Blue Tit, Coal Tit, Teal, Woodpigeon; R. J. Chandler: Tree Creeper; H. Clark: Ringed Plover; A. Cleave: 24 tr, 25 tr, 25 tr, Dog Whelk, Lugworm, Sea Anemne, Starfish; P. Craig-Cooper: Chaffinch; G. du Feau: Grey Plover; J. Hall: 13 tr, 20 br; P. Henderson: 13 brvi, Ostracod; E. A. Janes: X br, Coot, Little Grebe; K. Karlson: Nuthatch; W. Peaton: Roe Deer; J. Russell: Great Tit; D. Smith: Leech, Rock Pipit; D. Summers: 9 tri; J. M. Sutherland: 25 bl; R. Tidman: 20 c, Black-headed Gull, Common Tern, Grey Heron, Mute Swan, Sanwich Tern, Tawny owl; N. Wilmore: Freshwater Shrimp.
While every effort has been made to trace and acknowledge all copyright holders, we would like to apologize should any omissions have been made.

Magnifying Dish
Put creatures or plants in this dish to take a closer look.

Brush
You can gently sweep up tiny, delicate creatures with the brush without harming them.

CONTENTS

Insect Observatory
Hold the end of one tube close to a small bug. Use the other tube like a straw to safely capture the insect.

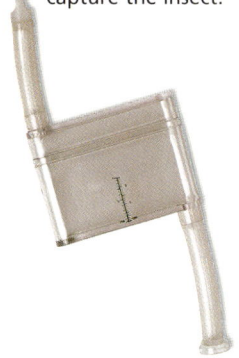

Tweezers
Use the tweezers to pick up creatures gently, or to sift through objects in your tray.

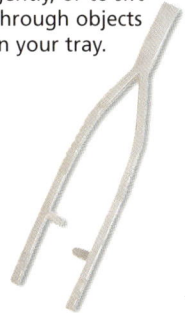

Naturalist's Tray
Fill your tray with leaf litter, earth, or mud. Spread your sample out and see what you can find.

FRESHWATER BIRDS
Gadwall
Size: 20 inches
Habitat: Ponds, marshes
Appearance: Black and white on wings
Behavior: Often in pairs

Black-and-White Sheet
Put the sheet under your naturalist's tray. Dark creatures will show up clearly against the light half and vice versa.

Animal Identifier Cards
Use these animal identifier cards, featuring woodland, freshwater, and seashore creatures, to help you recognize the creatures you spot.

Styles and colors may vary.

WOODLANDS

Woodland trees are home to birds, mammals, and insects. Some trees, such as pines and spruces, keep their leaves all year long. These are called conifers. Others, called broad-leaved trees, shed their leaves in the fall and do not grow new ones until the spring. In spring, flowers cover the woodland floor, attracting butterflies and other insects. Even the leafmold on the ground is full of amazing minibeasts.

Rot Spot

Trees sometimes lose branches or are blown over in a gale. The timber lies on the woodland floor until the wood eventually rots away. Look under a piece of rotting wood or peel back some bark to find a strange world of minibeasts to explore with your naturalist's kit. At any time of year, you will find slugs and snails under fallen logs. Look at one closely through your magnifying lid and try to see the breathing hole near the head.

Millipede

Common Slug

Centipede

Common Woodlouse

Centipedes, millipedes, and woodlice are also found here. They like damp conditions and can stay safe from predators such as birds. Look at the underside of the log. You may see holes made by beetle larvae living in the wood. Gently remove the strips of wood to see inside the creature's tunnel.

Use your tweezers to sort through rotten leaves and wood in your tray. When you have finished looking at a log, put it back in place gently.

Beetle Pupae

Tracks and Trails

There is evidence to show that many creatures have been in the woodland even when you cannot see them. Look for the droppings and footprints of foxes, deer, and birds along well-worn tracks.

Look, too, for branches covered in bird droppings. An owl may have roosted there. Search the ground for owl pellets. These are the remains of an owl's meal. Put the pellet in your tray, and pull it apart with your tweezers.

Make a collection of nibbled nuts. Using your magnifying lid, look for teeth marks in the edges.

Acorn nibbled by a squirrel.

Hazelnut nibbled by a deer mouse.

Hazelnut nibbled by a vole.

Minibeast Detective

Many woodland creatures stay hidden, and it takes some detective work to find them.

Leafmold on the woodland floor is home to many creatures. Push the surface leaves aside and use your insect observatory to collect tiny animals that you see moving. Springtails, false scorpions, centipedes, and tiny beetles are among the many types you will find.

Try putting some of the leafmold in your tray, shaking it from time to time. Any minibeasts will gradually move to the bottom of the tray.

Spread a large sheet under a tree or shrub, and tap one of the branches with a stick. Creatures will fall off the branch onto the sheet.

Use your tweezers and brush to transfer the creatures to the magnifying dish.

(1)

(2)

Tree Canopy

Many insects and birds live in the top layer of the woodland, called the tree canopy.

(3)

Each species of tree has different bark. Some are smooth, while others have deep cracks in the surface. Make bark rubbings to record them, using paper and a wax crayon. Keep each rubbing in a notebook with a leaf from the tree. This will help identify the tree.

(5)

(4)

(6)

(7)

Pine and spruce trees produce their seeds in cones. The seeds are found between the flaps that make up the cone. A few new trees grow from these seeds, but most are eaten by mice, squirrels, or other woodland creatures. Look for different cones and make a collection.

(8)

(9)

In most woodlands, you will come across cut-down trees. At the cut end, there are rings spreading out from the center. Each ring is made during a season's growth by the tree. Make a rubbing of the tree's rings with paper and a wax crayon. Count the number of rings to estimate the tree's age.

Woodland Floor

Many of the woodland's mammals live here. Fallen leaves carpet the ground, and flowers appear in the spring. Fungi bring color to the woodland floor in the fall.

(10)

Understory

Shrubs, bushes, and small trees grow in the understory, beneath the shade of the woodland's largest trees.

1 Long-Eared Owl
2 Pine Hawk Moth
3 Sharp-Shinned Hawk
4 Crossbill
5 Woodpecker
6 Whitetail Deer
7 Birch
8 Question Mark Butterfly
9 Kinglet
10 Earthworm
11 Black-Capped Chickadee
12 Brown Creeper
13 Nuthatch
14 Oak
15 Olive-Sided Flycatcher
16 Gray Squirrel
17 Bracken
18 Fly Agaric
19 Vole
20 Deer Mouse
21 Red Fox
22 Bumblebee
23 Shield Bug
24 Violet Wood Sorrel

GRASSLANDS

Grasslands and meadows are great places for a young naturalist to explore. Birds nest here and there, and butterflies and grasshoppers abound in the summer months among the grass and colorful flowers. Some of the animals are shy, and hide among the grass stems. A few even live secret lives at ground level or in the soil itself. Use the equipment in your naturalist's kit to help you track them down.

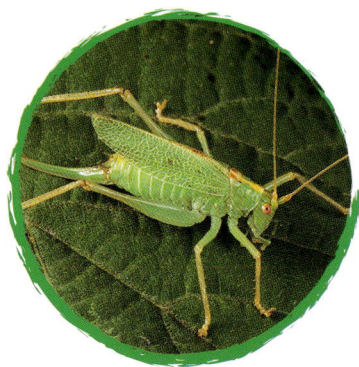

Bush crickets like this one have shorter bodies than grasshoppers, and larger antennae.

Down in the Grass

Find an open area among the tall grasses to investigate with your insect observatory. Get down on your hands and knees. Move slowly, keeping the nozzle close to the ground. Among the loose soil at the base of grass stems, you will find lots of tiny animals to suck up, such as young grasshoppers, plant bugs, small beetles, earwigs, and tiny flies. If you have a butterfly net, you can use it as a sweep net as well. Walk through the grass, sweeping from side to side. Put the contents of the net into your tray. Place the black-and-white sheet underneath the tray to help you sort the sample. These are some of the creatures you may find:

Soldier Beetle

Lacewing

Plant Bug

All Change

Egg

Butterflies start life as tiny eggs laid on plant leaves. Some butterflies lay the eggs singly. Others lay them in groups.

Swallowtails lay a single egg.

Caterpillar

After about a week, the eggs hatch into caterpillars. These eat the leaves of the plant. Now and then, the caterpillars shed their skins so that they can grow bigger.

Swallowtail caterpillars are brightly colored.

Chrysalis

When the caterpillar is fully grown, it turns into a chrysalis. You will find them hanging from leaves or in the soil.

The swallowtail chrysalis looks like a dried-up leaf.

Adult Butterfly

In the spring, a new butterfly emerges from the chrysalis. At first, its wings are soft and crumpled. They harden and dry in the air.

Most butterflies feed on flower nectar to give them energy. Watch them visit a meadow flower. They use a long tube, called a proboscis, to suck up the sugary liquid.

These tortoiseshell and question mark butterflies are feeding on nectar.

The adult swallowtail has distinctive black and yellow markings.

Bug Trap

Dig a trap in a place where people do not usually walk.

Leave enough room for creatures to crawl under the stone.

Check your trap and release the creatures every three to four hours.

Dig a small hole in the soil and bury a jar up to its rim. Cover the top of your trap with a stone or piece of wood to stop it from filling with rain. Prop up the lid with small stones. Examine the jar each day for creatures that have fallen in. Remove the jar when you have finished your experiment.

1

2

3

5

4

6

7

8

10

Understory

If you want to watch mammals and birds, creep around on hands and knees, using the grass as cover. If you sit quietly, you may be lucky enough to see voles and mice emerge from their burrows.

1	American Kestrel	9 American Copper
2	Queen Anne's Lace	10 Northern Harrier
3	Yarrow	11 Short-Eared Owl
4	Painted Lady	12 Oxeye Daisy
5	Least Weasel	13 Alfalfa Butterfly
6	Meadow Vole	14 Jackrabbit
7	Earthworm	15 Marsh Thistle
8	Mole	16 Fairy Ring Fungi
		17 Shrew
		18 Cranefly Larva

POND LIFE

At first glance, ponds may not seem ideal places to look for wildlife. Their water is still and shallow, and you will not usually hear loud bird or animal calls. But take a closer look. In fact, most ponds are teeming with life, from large animals like frogs and newts, to tiny insects such as diving beetles and pond skaters. Using your naturalist's kit— and your eyes and ears— you will be able to discover a wonderful, hidden world.

Gas Plants

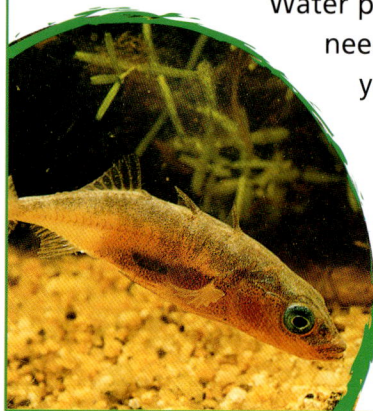

Water plants make oxygen, the gas that all living creatures need to breathe. You can watch this happening. Fill your magnifying dish with pond water, and put in a small piece of pondweed. Then place the dish on a sunny window ledge. In just a few minutes, you will see small bubbles of oxygen coming out of the leaves.

The oxygen made by pondweed dissolves in water. Fish and other underwater creatures can then absorb it through their gills.

Water Babies

The shimmering dragonflies that can be seen around most ponds started life as eggs laid in the water. These hatch into tiny nymphs. Visit your local pond on a spring morning, and you may see some fully-grown nymphs climbing up plant stems. Wait patiently and their skins will split open. Beautiful adult dragonflies will soon emerge, and then fly away before midday. Pick up one of the empty skins and put it into your magnifying dish. If you look carefully, you will see some tiny white threads. These are the tubes that the nymph breathed through.

All adult dragonflies have four fine-veined wings, which rub together noisily as they fly along.

Dragonfly nymphs spend several months in the water before climbing out.

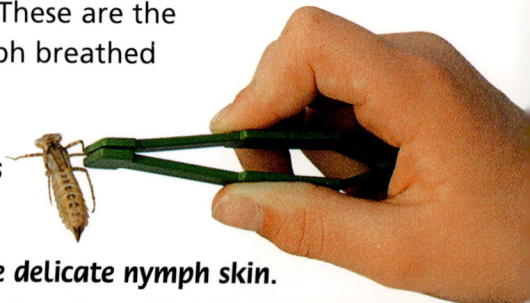

Use your special tweezers to pick up the delicate nymph skin.

Grow Your Own Frog

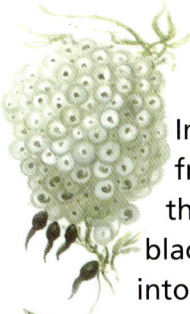

In the spring, one of the easiest things to find in a pond is frogspawn. Female frogs lay these sticky masses of eggs around the edges where the water is shallow. Each egg looks like a small black dot and is surrounded by jelly. You can watch the spawn grow into frogs. Scoop a small amount into a bucket and take it home.

Transfer the spawn to a tank filled with pond water. Put in some pondweed and small freshwater creatures, as your tadpoles will need these to live on. Remember to change the water once a week, using rainwater. Slowly, the dots inside the jelly will change shape. After about a week, tiny tadpoles will hatch out.

The black dots in the spawn gradually turn into comma-shaped tadpoles.

When they first hatch, tadpoles eat the remains of their own eggs.

Tadpoles grow back legs first, then front legs.

Miraculous Mud

The slimy mud at the bottom of ponds is full of life. You simply need to look for it. First, take a small scoop of mud and put it in your naturalist's tray. Then slide the black-and-white sheet underneath. Light-colored animals will show up against the black half, and dark-colored animals against the white. Next, fill your magnifying dish with clean water and gently transfer the animals to it, one at a time. These are some of the creatures you may find:

Freshwater Shrimp   **Pea Mussel**   **Leech**

Water Flea   **Freshwater Worm**   **Ostracod**

Use a plastic spoon to transfer animals from tray to dish.

You only need a small amount of mud to find a wide variety of creatures.

1

2

3

4

5

Water Surface

Air and water meet at the surface of the pond, and the water forms a fragile skin. Many animals come to the surface to breathe air.

7

6

Water Column

This is the main part of the water, below the surface. Here you can find plants and a wide variety of creatures, from water scorpions to schools of fish.

8

You can trap newts and other pond animals in a net. But always put them back in the pond again!

9

10

11
15

12

13
14

Pond Margin

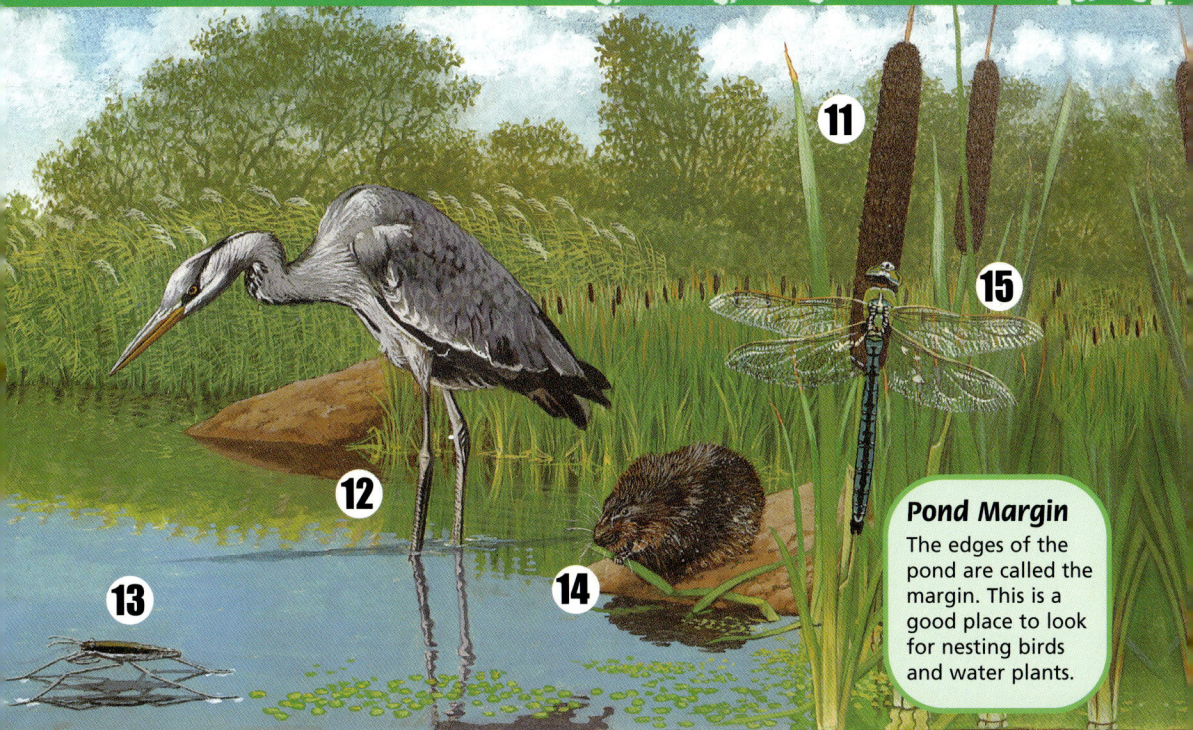

The edges of the pond are called the margin. This is a good place to look for nesting birds and water plants.

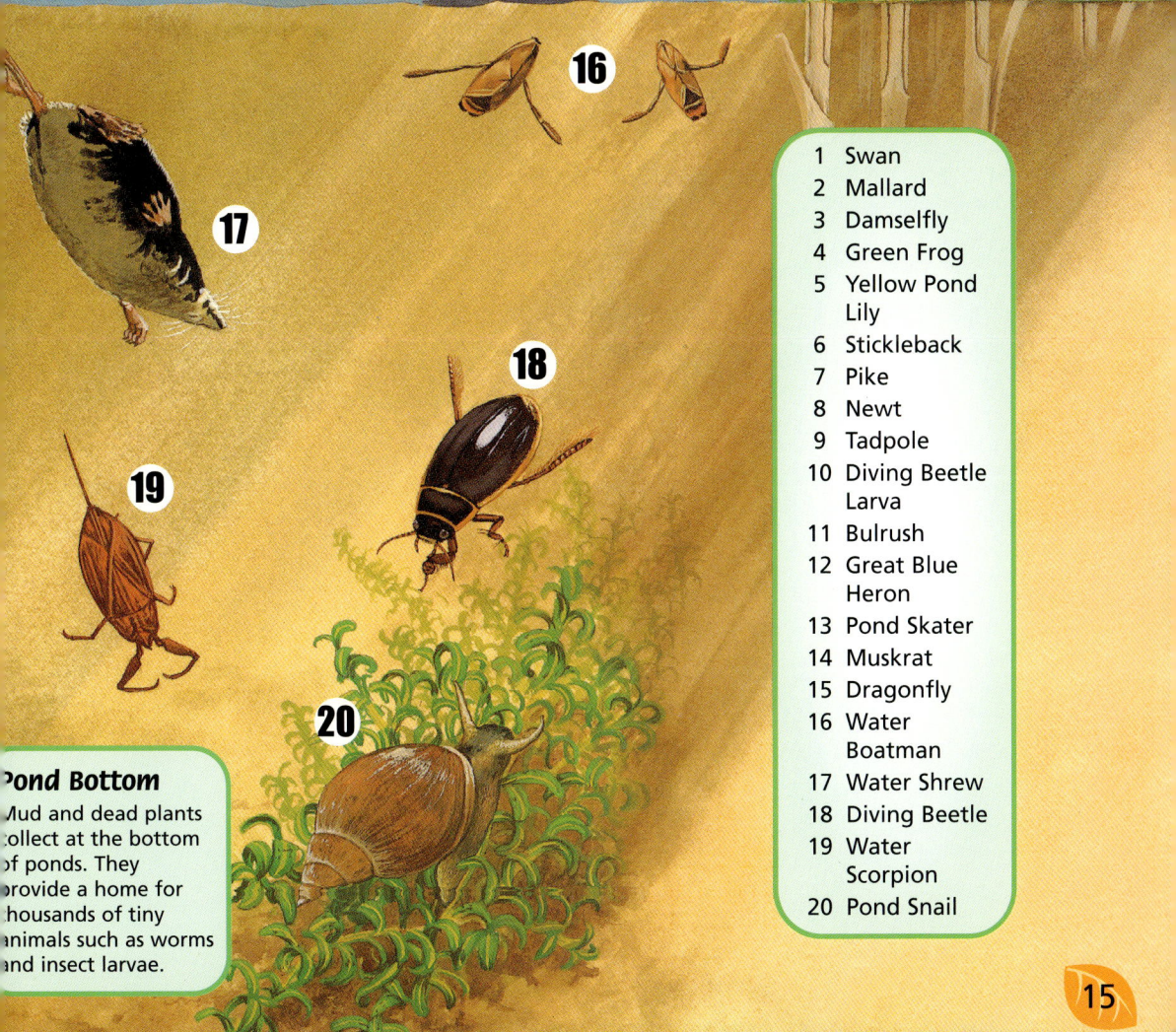

16

17

18

19

20

1 Swan
2 Mallard
3 Damselfly
4 Green Frog
5 Yellow Pond Lily
6 Stickleback
7 Pike
8 Newt
9 Tadpole
10 Diving Beetle Larva
11 Bulrush
12 Great Blue Heron
13 Pond Skater
14 Muskrat
15 Dragonfly
16 Water Boatman
17 Water Shrew
18 Diving Beetle
19 Water Scorpion
20 Pond Snail

Pond Bottom

Mud and dead plants collect at the bottom of ponds. They provide a home for thousands of tiny animals such as worms and insect larvae.

RIVERS AND STREAMS

Small, fast-flowing streams grow into broader, slower rivers. Plants and animals living there have to survive in flowing water without getting washed away. Plants anchor themselves to the bottom. Some animals can swim well, but some attach themselves to the plants, or to rocks and stones.

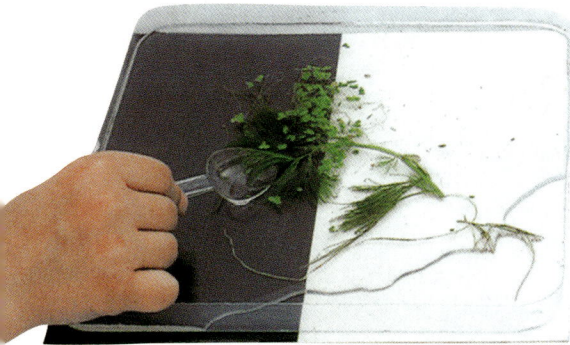

Scoop up small amounts of river weed to examine in your naturalist's tray.

Stream Scooping

Flowing water means that many creatures may get washed away before you can catch them in your net. Try placing a net on the downstream side of a stone and then lifting the stone's edge. Crayfish, freshwater shrimp, and other creatures will try to escape, but will swim straight into the net. Many of the creatures live in the mud, sand, or gravel at the bottom. Living here stops them from being washed away and protects them from predators such as hungry fish. Scoop up a small sample using the net, and place it in your tray with the black-and-white sheet underneath.

Many of the creatures have soft bodies and are easily damaged. Using a plastic spoon, transfer them to the magnifying dish in your naturalist's kit for a closer look. Remember to return the creatures to the water as soon as you have finished looking at them. Many of them need flowing water to breathe properly and will die if kept for too long.

Great Pond Snail

Mayfly Larva

Damselfly Nymph

Adult Damselfly

Mobile Homes

Caddisflies are common along most rivers and streams. The young, called caddisfly larvae, live in water. They live in cases made from twigs, sand, or even tiny snail shells all glued together. The case protects the animal's soft body. To find caddisfly larvae, dredge a small amount of weed and silt from a river and place it in your tray with some water. After a few minutes, the larvae will begin to move, dragging their homes around with them. If you watch closely, you may see one repair its home.

This caddisfly larva has a case made from pieces of plant.

Eye Spy

Fish can see you on the bank of the river long before you see them. Water bends light, like a lens or a prism, giving the fish a good view of the river bank.

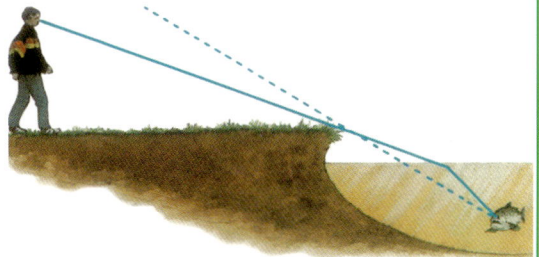

If the river contained no water, light would travel in a straight line, so the fish would not see you.

In fact, light bends at the water's surface, so the fish can see you.

How Fast is the Flow?

To measure the speed of a river, you will need a helper. First, measure a 30-foot (10 meter) stretch of river bank with a tape measure, and mark both ends with a stick. One person should drop an orange into the water at the upstream marker. The other person times how long it takes for the orange to reach the second marker. Use a stopwatch or the second hand on your wristwatch. Catch the orange with your net at the end of the experiment. Compare the water speed here with tests on other rivers, or try the experiment on the bend of a river, too.

A river flows at about 2mph (3km/h). A fast stream may reach 6mph (10km/h). In a slow river, your orange should take 12 seconds to travel the distance. In a fast stream, it may take 4 seconds.

Faster parts of the river tend to have fewer plants and animals living in them.

River Safety

- Wear waterproof boots or old sneakers when you wade and never wade out too far.
- Always go with an adult.
- Watch out for water snakes—they can be dangerous.

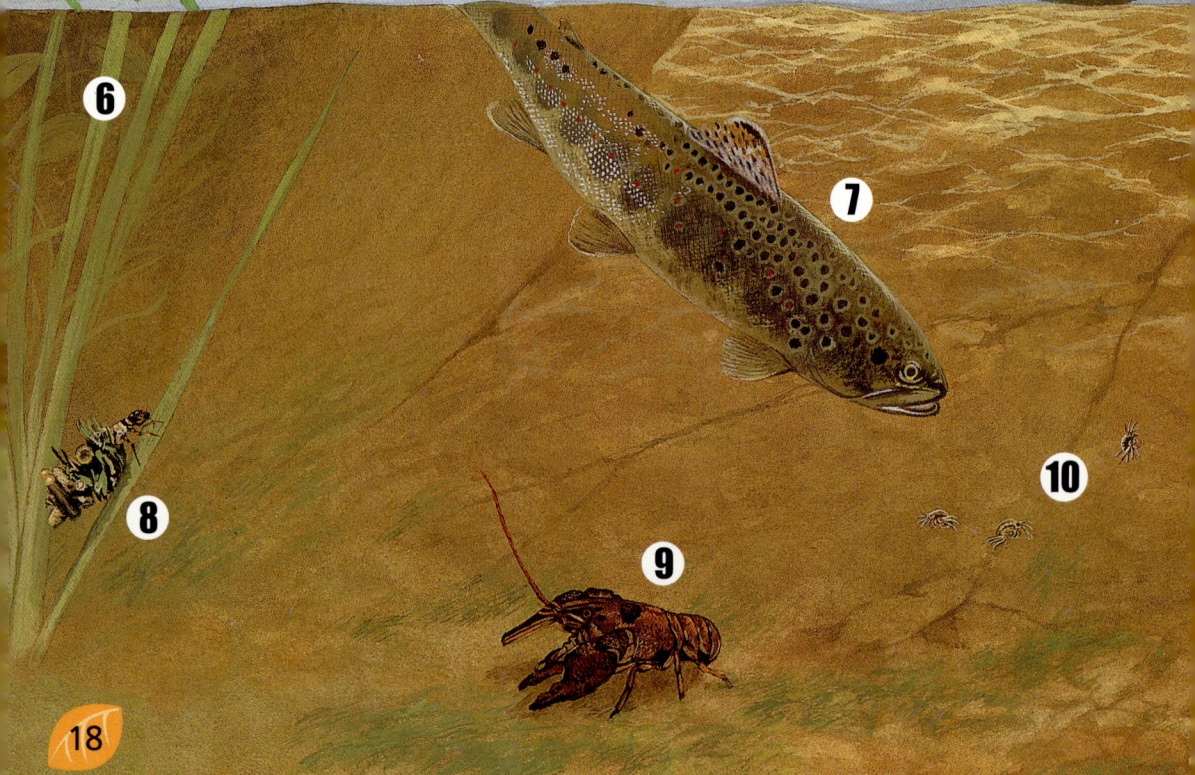

Mayflies spend most of their lives as larvae in water. In April or May, the adults emerge and fly for a few days before mating, laying eggs, and dying. The males fly in swarms over the water waiting for females to arrive. Visit a river on a warm spring evening to see them.

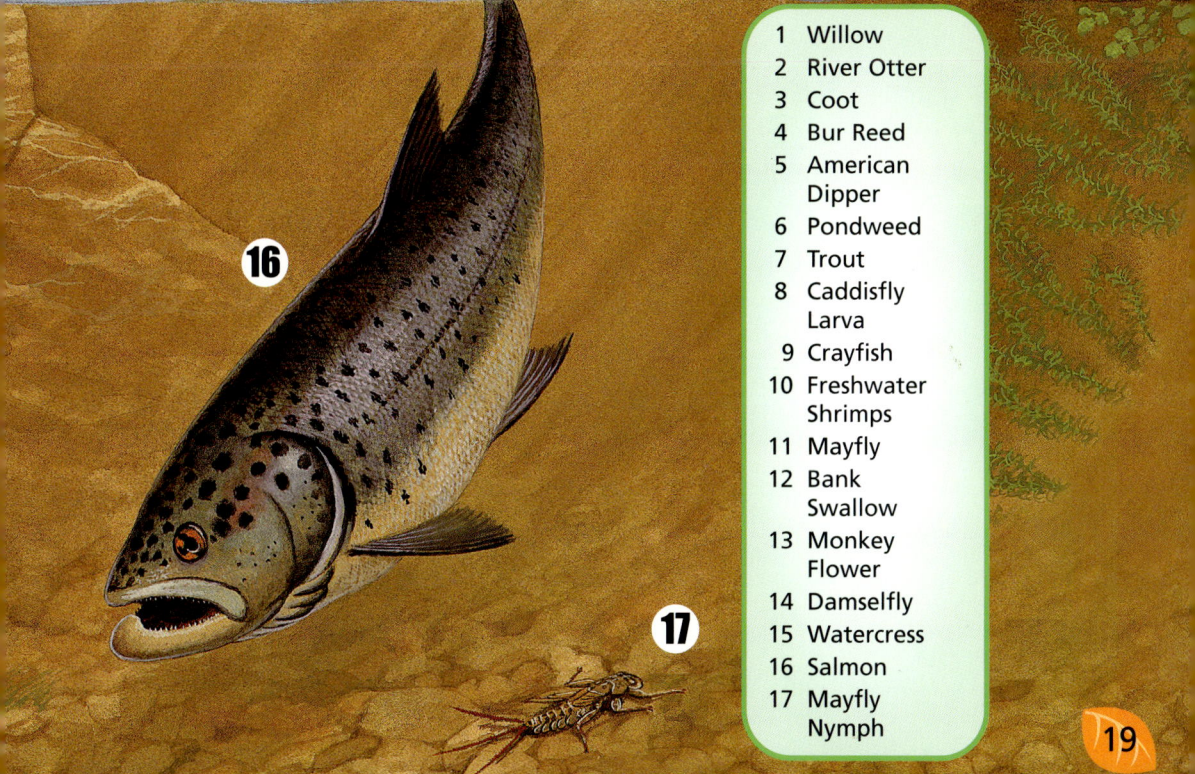

1 Willow
2 River Otter
3 Coot
4 Bur Reed
5 American Dipper
6 Pondweed
7 Trout
8 Caddisfly Larva
9 Crayfish
10 Freshwater Shrimps
11 Mayfly
12 Bank Swallow
13 Monkey Flower
14 Damselfly
15 Watercress
16 Salmon
17 Mayfly Nymph

BOGS AND MARSHES

Bogs and marshes are places where land and water meet. The soil is always waterlogged, and there are plenty of pools and areas of open water. Wetland plants thrive in these habitats, and many colorful and interesting species can be found. Ducks and secretive water-birds can breed safely in the cover of dense vegetation, while waterbugs, water beetles, and dragonfly nymphs fill the water itself.

Show-Down

Many birds choose sheltered marshes to breed in the spring. As part of their courtship, they may show unusual behavior. Snipe have a special display flight. They fan their tail feathers as they dive through the air. The feathers vibrate in the wind and produce a loud drumming sound. Male moorhens fight each other, using their powerful legs and long toes to push their opponent underwater.

The snipe's long bill is ideal for digging deep in the mud for food.

Moorhens' thin feet make them good fighters. However, webbed feet are better for swimming.

Spawn Strings

In the spring, toads return to marshy pools and bogs to breed. Just like frogs, their eggs are protected by jelly. However, the eggs are produced in long strings rather than masses like frogspawn. The strings are wrapped around the stems of water plants. Collect some toadspawn and look at the eggs in your magnifying dish. You will see the developing tadpoles.

Most toads have dry, warty skin, unlike frogs which have smooth, wet skin.

Female toads like to lay their spawn in deep water.

Meat-Eaters

Most plants get all the food they need from the soil and from sunlight energy. However, a few bog and marsh plants such as sundews and bladderworts get extra food by catching and eating small animals. The underwater stems of the bladderwort produce small bladders, each with a trapdoor. Tiny pond animals get caught and are digested within the bladders. Sundews trap insects on their sticky leaves.

Enzymes on sundew leaves digest the insects so that the plant can absorb them. Use your magnifying lid to look for insect remains on sundew leaves.

A bladderwort stem stretches out of the water.

Beneath the water are the bladders.

This enlarged section shows a small creature captured inside a bladder.

Insect Helpers

Purple loosestrife has colorful flowers in July and August that attract waterside insects. The insects visit the flowers to collect nectar, but they also carry pollen from one flower to another, which helps the flowers to produce seeds.

Use your magnifying lid to see the pollen grains sticking to the bees, flies, and other insects on the flowers. Do not touch bees or wasps as they may sting you.

Air Bubbles

Although they spend most of their lives under water, water beetles still breathe air. Many of them carry a bubble of air beneath their wing cases or trapped in hairs on their bodies. Catch one and put it in your magnifying dish or insect observatory pot with some water. Look at it through the side, and you will see the silvery bubble of air. Now and then, beetles have to return to the surface of the water to replace the air. Most do this by sticking their tail end and the end of their wing cases through the surface of the water.

Put the beetle back in the water carefully when you have finished looking at it.

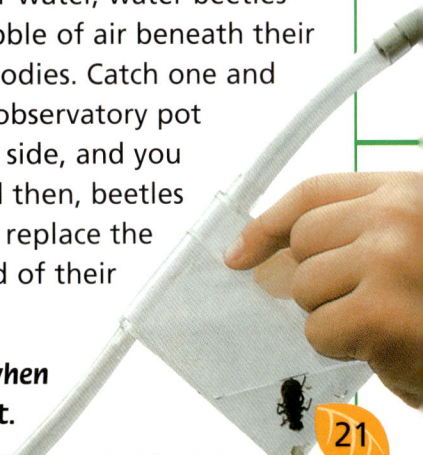

1 Canada Goose
2 Cattail
3 Dragonfly
4 American Bittern
5 Virginia Rail
6 Water Smartweed
7 Giant Reed
8 Pintail
9 Marsh Marigold
10 Bladderwort
11 Water Stick Insect
12 Water Snail
13 Sphagnum Moss
14 Willow
15 Alder
16 Purple Loosestrife
17 Damsefly
18 Cottongrass
19 Horsetail
20 Gadwall
21 Marsh Fern
22 Moorhen
23 Marestail
24 Snipe
25 Toad
26 Round-Leaved Sundew
27 Butterwort

Bitterns live in dense reedbeds, where they feed on frogs and fish. When they are alarmed, they stretch their necks to make themselves tall and thin. The markings on their feathers help them blend in with the reeds.

The long, thin body of the water stick insect gives it good camouflage among the stems of water plants. It lies in wait for passing prey, which it catches with its pincerlike front legs.

Marsh Safety

Bogs and marshes can be dangerous places, so always tread carefully or visit an area with a boardwalk.

15

Damselflies and dragonflies are common around bogs and marshes. To tell them apart, watch them settle. Damselflies hold their wings folded over their backs. Dragonflies keep their wings spread out flat.

14

18

17

16

19

21

22

20

23

24

25

26

27

SEASHORES

Explore the seashore and you will find some strange animals and plants, quite unlike those in a pond or river. The seashore is the place where the land and the sea meet. The tide rises and falls, covering and uncovering the shore, so animals and plants have to be able to live in salty seawater as well as air. Crabs scuttle under stones for cover, while the rocks are covered in limpets, barnacles, sea anemones, and seaweeds.

Clams have two hinged shells.

Shell Search

Razorshells can dig with their shells faster than a person using their hands.

Seashells were once the homes of seashore mollusks, relatives of slugs and snails. Along a sandy beach or the tidemark of a rocky shore, you will find shells of all different sizes and shapes. Be sure to collect only empty shells. Try to guess where the mollusk lived when it was alive by looking at the shape of the shell. Cone-shaped limpets attach themselves to flat rocks, while cockles and razorshells bury themselves in the sand, pushing through it with their sharp edges.

Limpets attach themselves to the rocks with a suckerlike foot.

Beachcombing

Twice a day, the tide rushes in and out, leaving all sorts of things washed up in a line known as the tidemark. Look out for mermaid's purses, which are the egg cases of dogfish, and cuttlebones, which are all that remain of cuttlefish when they die. Driftwood may be covered with animals called goose barnacles. The best time to go beachcombing is after a gale. All sorts of strange things are washed up. Sadly, because many seas are polluted, oil and tar is often washed up on the shore as well. Be sure not to get any on your hands or clothes.

KELP

BLADDER WRACK

SPIRAL WRACK

SERRATED WRACK

CUTTLEBONE

MERMAIDS PURSE

Keep a beach diary with drawings of all the things you see.

All Washed Up

Rock pools are ideal places to study the seashore with your naturalist's kit. You can find animals such as crabs, blennies, starfish, and periwinkles. After each tide, the water in the rock pool is replaced, and new animals are washed in by the waves.

Use a small net to catch the creatures and place them in your naturalist's tray with some seawater. Place the black-and-white card underneath, and move it around to see the animals better.

Blennies can be hard to catch as they hide in crevices in the rock.

A Gripping Tale

Gently turn a live starfish on its back in your naturalist's tray. You will see thousands of tiny suckers along each of its arms. The starfish uses these to move and feed. It grips the two halves of a mussel's shell and slowly pulls them apart to reach the animal inside.

Put the starfish upright again and watch it move. It can move just as easily in any direction.

Try putting a live mussel in the tray with the starfish. You may be able to watch the starfish eat.

If a starfish loses an arm, it can grow a new one. A whole new starfish can grow from the severed piece of arm, too.

Hermit Homes

Hermit crabs do not have a hard shell like other crabs. They protect themselves by living inside empty seashells. When the crab grows too big, it has to search for a larger home. You may be able to watch this if you put a hermit crab in your naturalist's tray with some empty shells. The crab may choose another shell as its new home.

Hermit crabs often pick whelk shells as their homes.

Watch a group of gulls on the seashore. A few gulls have a special way of feeding on mollusks with hard shells. They fly up high, carrying the mollusk, and then drop it onto the rocks. The shell smashes, and then the gull can get its meal.

1

2

3

4

5

6

7

8

9

1	Herring Gull
2	Seaside Spurge
3	Semi-Palmated Plover
4	Sanderling
5	Great Black-Backed Gull
6	Shore Crab
7	Clam
8	Razorshell
9	Sandhopper
10	Common Tern
11	Sea Sandwort
12	Beach Grass
13	Harbor Seal
14	Oystercatcher
15	Mussel
16	Whelk
17	Barnacle
18	Limpet
19	Anemone
20	Blenny
21	Starfish

27

TOWNS AND BACKYARDS

Although gardeners try to keep nature under control, there is still plenty of wildlife to be found right under your nose in your own backyard. Use your naturalist's kit to find minibeasts in the yard soil, or watch insects and birds visiting the yard to feed. You can even encourage wildlife to come to your backyard by trying to create the right kind of environment.

The spider leaves a few dry threads in the center of the web to sit on.

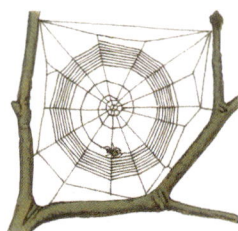

Web Weaving

Watch for a spider beginning to weave its web.

1. It starts by attaching silk strands to three fixed objects.

2. Next, it makes radiating strands like the spokes of a bicycle wheel.

3. Then, it spins a temporary spiral of dry thread around the web to hold it together. Finally, the spider spins a spiral of sticky thread working back towards the center of the web, eating the dry thread as it goes. Flies and other insects get caught in the sticky strands of the web.

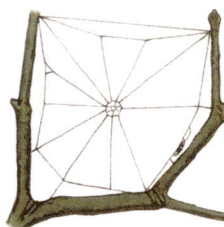

The Gardener's Friend

Earthworms are among the most useful creatures in the yard. They burrow in the ground and mix air in with the soil. They also drag leaves and other plant remains into their burrows. This adds nutrients to the soil like a natural fertilizer. Look for worm casts on the surface of the soil.

Put a worm in your tray with some leafmold. Watch how it moves by relaxing and contracting its body.

Earthworms may live in tunnels as deep as 6 feet under the soil.

The Gardener's Enemies

Some of the most fascinating and common creatures are considered to be pests by gardeners.

Although they move slowly, snails travel a considerable distance each night. Try tracking their progress. Mark a few snail shells with nail polish. Draw a map of your yard. Search for the marked snails each morning in hiding places under flowerpots or stones. Plot their movements on your map.

Snails love to eat young plant shoots.

You can find ants in most yards. They live in underground colonies, in a system of tunnels and chambers. You can watch the comings and goings at the colony entrance using your magnifying lid. The ants move away from the entrance using special tracks. They follow these using their sense of smell. Put an obstacle in an ant's path. How long does it take to get around it? Occasionally, an ant will return with some food for the colony. It might be a dead insect or a piece of plant material.

Each summer, when the colony becomes too big, large numbers of ants leave to form a new colony.

Ants sometimes go into houses looking for sugary foods.

Mushrooms and Toadstools

Fall is the season for fungi, which we usually call mushrooms and toadstools. Several different types may appear on your lawn or in your flowerbeds. Instead of seeds, they produce spores from gills underneath their caps. Cut the cap off a toadstool. Place it on a sheet of white paper and leave overnight. When you lift the toadstool cap, you will see an impression of its gills, made by the fallen spores. Remember that a few fungi are poisonous, so always wash your hands after making a spore print.

Some fungi are brown or gray. Others are red, orange, or patterned.

Lift the toadstool cap off carefully. You can cover your print with plastic wrap, or spray varnish over it.

In winter, birds have to eat well to keep warm, but food is difficult to find. You can attract birds to your yard by putting out extra food for them. Each species has its own favorites:
Peanuts: chickadees, greenfinches, woodpeckers
Fat and lard: woodpeckers, starlings, nuthatches
Grain: pigeons, finches, thrushes
Bread: thrushes, starlings

You can help wildlife by turning part of your backyard into a special wildlife garden. A small pond in the yard is a good way to encourage frogs and birds to come to drink and bathe. Some plants have flowers that are particularly attractive to insects. If you want lots of butterflies in your yard, plant buddleias, iceplants, or New England asters. Try not to use pesticides or insecticides unless you really have to. These often kill off useful creatures as well as harmful ones.

1 Starling
2 Cabbage White
3 Feral Pigeon
4 House Sparrow
5 Red Admiral
6 House Fly
7 Frog
8 House Mouse
9 Wasp
10 Earthworm
11 Tortoiseshell
12 Sphinx Moth
13 Honey Bee
14 Ladybug
15 Ant

THE FOUR SEASONS

In North America and Europe, the weather changes throughout the year. We have four seasons. These are spring, summer, fall and winter. There are different things to look out for in each season.

Spring

Spring is a time of growth and new life. Look out for young plants and animals.

Summer

In summer, many plants flower. The air is full of buzzing insects. Look out for dragonflies and butterflies.

Fall

Many plants produce nuts and fruit in the fall. How many different types can you find?

Winter

In winter, broad-leaved trees are bare. Some insects and animals find a warm place to hibernate until spring.